WEEKLY **WR** READER®

EARLY LEARNING LIBRARY

How People Lived in America

Food and Cooking in American History

by Dana Meachen Rau

Reading consultant:
Susan Nations, M.Ed.,
author/literacy coach/
consultant in literacy development

Please visit our web site at: www.garethstevens.com
For a free color catalog describing Weekly Reader® Early Learning Library's list
of high-quality books, call 1-877-445-5824 (USA) or 1-800-387-3178 (Canada).
Weekly Reader® Early Learning Library's fax: (414) 336-0164.

Library of Congress Cataloging-in-Publication Data

Rau, Dana Meachen, 1971-
    Food and cooking in American history / by Dana Meachen Rau.
        p. cm. — (How people lived in America)
    Includes bibliographical references and index.
    ISBN-10: 0-8368-7206-1 — ISBN-13: 978-0-8368-7206-4 (lib. bdg.)
    ISBN-10: 0-8368-7213-4 — ISBN-13: 978-0-8368-7213-2 (softcover)
    1. Cookery, American—History—Juvenile literature. 2. Food—History—Juvenile literature. I. Title.
    TX715.R2375   2006
    641.5973—dc22   2006008629

This edition first published in 2007 by
Weekly Reader® Early Learning Library
A Member of the WRC Media Family of Companies
330 West Olive Street, Suite 100
Milwaukee, WI 53212 USA

Copyright © 2007 by Weekly Reader® Early Learning Library

Editor: Barbara Kiely Miller
Art direction: Tammy West
Cover design and page layout: Kami Strunsee
Picture research: Sabrina Crewe

Picture credits: Cover, title page © Swim Ink 2/CORBIS; p. 4 © Michelle D. Bridwell/PhotoEdit;
pp. 6, 7, 8, 11, 12, 17, 19 The Granger Collection, New York; pp. 9, 14, 15 16 © North Wind Picture
Archives; p. 10 © Lee Snider/CORBIS; p. 13 © Medford Historical Society Collection/CORBIS; p. 18
© CORBIS; p. 20 © Bettmann/CORBIS; p. 21 © Michael Newman/PhotoEdit

Printed in the United States of America

1 2 3 4 5 6 7 8 9 10 09 08 07 06

Table of Contents

Cover: Large, iron stoves stood in the kitchens of many American homes in the early 1900s.

A microwave oven cooks and heats up food much faster than a stove.

Food and Cooking Today

Today, people buy fresh meat, fruits, and vegetables at stores. Then they keep the food in **refrigerators** and cook it on stoves. But long ago, people had to hunt for their own meat. They had to grow their own fruits and vegetables. They cooked their food over a fire. Gathering and cooking food was hard work.

Long ago, people . . .

- did not have grocery stores;
- did not have refrigerators or freezers;
- did not cook on stoves;
- did not have sinks with running water;
- did not have microwave ovens;
- did not eat in restaurants;
- did not eat food from cans;
- did not use forks.

Food in Early America

Early **settlers** came to America from Europe in the 1600s. Native Americans taught them how to grow new foods. The Native people taught the settlers how to grow corn, squash, beans, and pumpkins. They even taught them how to make popcorn!

Settlers cut down trees to make room for fields of corn. They learned to grow corn from Native Americans.

Men hunted for deer and wild turkeys in the woods. Settlers who lived near the ocean caught lobsters, crabs, and other seafood. Many people farmed or planted gardens for fresh vegetables. Some people had **orchards** of apples or peach trees.

Men spent a lot of time hunting and fishing. The settlers ate small animals, fish, and some birds.

A small oven was built into the brick or stone next to a fireplace. Women baked bread in the oven.

Women cooked all the meals for their families. They used large stone fireplaces to cook. The women put food in iron cooking pots that hung over the flames. They gathered wood to keep the fires going. Women had to collect water from nearby streams or **wells**, too.

Early Americans ate their biggest meal in the middle of the day. This meal was usually a **stew** of meat and vegetables served with bread. Women made butter in **butter churns**. Most people did not own forks. They ate with spoons or their fingers!

Everyone in a family gathered together to eat a big meal and talk.

The settlers did not have refrigerators. They used other ways to keep food fresh or **preserve** it. They added salt to some foods. They dried meat with smoke. They dried berries and vegetables, too. They made fruit into jam. To keep food cold, people stored it in a room below the house called a **cellar**.

This brick "root cellar" was built into the side of a hill in 1756. It was built under part of a house.

Keeping Food Fresh

In the 1800s, people bought food from a general store. But they still baked bread and churned butter at home. They cooked their food on iron stoves that burned wood. **Water pumps** brought water for cooking and cleaning right into the house.

People could buy goods, see friends, and get news at their town's store.

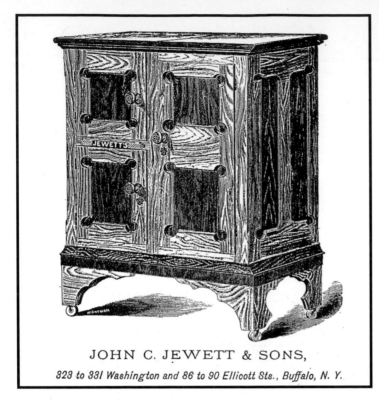

JOHN C. JEWETT & SONS,

323 to 331 Washington and 86 to 90 Ellicott Sts., Buffalo, N. Y.

This wooden icebox has three doors. The ice was kept behind one door. Food was stored on shelves behind the other doors.

Iceboxes now kept food fresh longer. An icebox was a cabinet made of wood. An iceman brought ice to the house. A block of ice was put in the icebox with the food. The ice melted slowly and kept the food cold.

Trains began crossing the country in the mid-1800s. They carried heavy loads of food and supplies. Some train cars were refrigerated. They kept meat, vegetables, and fruit cold. Food could now be brought from far away and still be fresh.

Food was shipped on special train cars called **freight** cars. The food was unloaded at a railroad yard.

Each night during their trip west, families camped next to their wagons. They made dinner over an open fire.

More people wanted to live in the western part of the country. In the 1840s, many families moved west in wagons. The trip took many months. People had to take along enough food. They packed bacon, beans, coffee, and flour.

In the late 1800s, cowboys moved large herds of cattle across open land in the West. The cowboys traveled with a **chuck wagon**. Chuck wagons were like traveling kitchens. Herding cattle was tough work. At the end of the day, the chuck wagon cook made hot, filling meals for the cowboys.

A chuck wagon cook made meals for cowboys who worked on a ranch, too.

People used baskets to carry food when shopping in a Piggly Wiggly.

Quick and Easy

Shopping for food became faster and easier in the 1900s. In 1916, a Piggly Wiggly store opened in Tennessee. In the past, people gave their shopping list to a clerk in a store. The clerk would collect the items. But in the Piggly Wiggly, people could walk through the aisles. They picked out their groceries themselves.

By the 1920s, many kitchens had a refrigerator. In 1923, a man named Clarence Birdseye invented a way to freeze food while it was still fresh. People could buy frozen food at the store and keep it frozen for months. People no longer had to burn wood in a stove to cook. By the 1930s, they cooked on gas and electric stoves. In the 1960s, people began heating food in **microwave ovens**.

New inventions made cooking more fun. Some children helped their mothers cook!

Drive-ins served hamburgers, French fries, and soft drinks.

In the 1950s, fast-food restaurants opened on busy roads. People driving in their cars could stop at the restaurants to eat. They could also buy meals there to take with them. Drive-in restaurants opened, too. At drive-ins, people sat in their cars, and servers brought food out to them. People could eat quickly and then be on their way!

Finding and cooking food is much easier today than it was long ago. Today, people can call a restaurant and have a pizza brought right to their house. Many years ago, there were no telephones, no cars, and no pizza! The ways that people can cook and eat have changed a lot over the last four hundred years!

Pizza is one kind of food that can be delivered to homes fast.

Glossary

butter churns — hand-powered machines that turn milk into butter

chuckwagon — a wagon that carried food and supplies for cooking meals for cowboys

microwave ovens — small ovens that cook food quickly using waves of energy

orchards — land where fruit trees are grown

preserve — to protect food from going bad so it can be eaten later

restaurants — places where people can buy meals that are ready to eat

settlers — people who move to and develop a new area

spicy — made with vegetables or other plants that have lots of flavor or taste hot

stew — meat and vegetables boiled together slowly in water or another liquid

water pumps — machines used to move water from one place to another

wells — deep holes in the ground used to bring a liquid, such as water, to the surface

For More Information

Books

Clarence Birdseye. Lives and Times (series). Tiffany Peterson (Heinemann)

Food in Grandma's Day. Valerie Weber and Jeraldine Jackson (Carolrhoda Books)

Pioneer Recipes. Historic Communities (series). Bobbie Kalman and Lynda Hale (Crabtree)

Web Site

Frontier House: Frontier Life
www.pbs.org/wnet/frontierhouse/frontierlife/essay6.html
Learn what pioneers on America's frontier ate and how they cooked it.

Publisher's note to educators and parents: Our editors have carefully reviewed this Web site to ensure that it is suitable for children. Many Web sites change frequently, however, and we cannot guarantee that a site's future contents will continue to meet our high standards of quality and educational value. Be advised that children should be closely supervised whenever they access the Internet.

Index

About the Author

Dana Meachen Rau is the author of more than one hundred and fifty children's books, including nonfiction and books for early readers. She writes about history, science, geography, people, and even toys! She lives with her family in Burlington, Connecticut.